DAVID BEN EKE

STRONG

DAVID BEN EKE

STRONG

...an unforgettable experience

JustFiction Edition

Imprint
Any brand names and product names mentioned in this book are subject to trademark, brand or patent protection and are trademarks or registered trademarks of their respective holders. The use of brand names, product names, common names, trade names, product descriptions etc. even without a particular marking in this work is in no way to be construed to mean that such names may be regarded as unrestricted in respect of trademark and brand protection legislation and could thus be used by anyone.

Cover image: www.ingimage.com

Publisher:
JustFiction! Edition
is a trademark of
International Book Market Service Ltd., member of OmniScriptum Publishing Group
17 Meldrum Street, Beau Bassin 71504, Mauritius
Printed at: see last page
ISBN: 978-620-3-57470-8

FOREWORD

Our Immediate society is one that contains people with wrong ideologies concerning women. This has enhanced many problems in our continent, Africa, and all over the world; ranking from rape, to female circumcision, and many more. Speaking of women's emancipation has been called something of impure reason, when it is actually a just course. It is something that moves for proper equality, justice, and freedom. Though many involved could make mistakes in feminism and what it entails, there is always an opportunity to learn!

This book is dedicated to the many young girls out there that are ready to make changes to the narrative of our system.

TABLE OF CONTENTS

CHAPTER ONE

Oroma answered the question confidently. She was very sure of her answer although it was believed in her school that no one could be so sure about this kind of things.

"Guy you asked if girls face trauma after rape. Well, for me it's weak girls that go through that, but it doesn't change the fact that rape is bad and should be grossly avoided", Oroma said with a personal fulfillment to have proved a point while answering Tony's question. He was Ada's boyfriend, and she was interloping into couples conversations as usual in class. Once she was done interloping, she'd walk to her own chair and sit like a lonely queen without a boyfriend.

She had come out today with her usual boldness, and what most crown students called;" an obviously shown disgust for boys". But that's only what they thought. She didn't actually hate boys. She was simply misunderstood because she out rightly spoke against even the slightest show of misogyny. She was a girl not to be messed with. She knew who she was, and what she wanted. She tagged along with the usual girly gang that walked together with a #ferminist high shoulder. Many students in Crown school found them weird because they talked about the most unlikely topics for teens to be talking about. It frightened many boys though; especially the ones who acted excessively superior in manners of speech and reasoning. They'd usually say to themselves that they had the rights to beat girls and talk to them however they liked, but when they were around Oroma and her girls, they lost their wrong morale. Oroma and her friends spoke against hard issues in Nigerian societies concerning women such as rape, female circumcision, early marriage, etc. They believed they possessed power over these and could make a change. It was already oroma's dream to be a die-hard lawyer, who would kill all these wrongs.

She never failed to tell herself everyday that she was a strong girl. She believed to be strong involved never crying in front of people, especially boys. She believed to be strong was to not face trauma or its relatives after a rape incident. She was too dogged about her personal notions. She needed to learn.

It was a Tuesday, and they had History. Senior WAEC was around the corner, so everyone paid rapid attention to Mr. Aja in class. Unlike before where everyone would be sleeping while Oroma argued intermittently with the teacher, everyone was seriously listening. The exams coming their way made them more keen to learn and be focused in class. Today they were learning about the role of women in precolonial times. As far as she was concerned, the teacher would make a mistake by saying something demeaning about women. He didn't beat her thoughts when he said;

 "Don't mind our women of nowadays, they don't want to stay in the kitchen 24/7. They don't know that is all they're good for."

His words vexed Oroma as usual. The other members of her feminist gang were science students, and she always had to face Mr. Aja alone. He spoke without watching his words most times, and she knew that. She only wondered how his wife managed him. He was over 65years, and he kept on making this kind of statements. She personally believed that where ever his grown up daughters were, they were cooking and cleaning, and doing nothing else. Oroma raised her hand.

"yes", Mr Aja said in response to her.

"Sir, please may I say something?", she asked politely. Everyone in the class already knew where she was driving at, and Mr Aja was in big trouble.

"Yes, you can", Mr Aja said.

She stood up from her chair, and closed the notebook that was open in front of her.

"Sir, what wrong have the women of our time done in trying to fend for themselves and their families. From all you've taught us and from what I know, a man is no better than a woman. There have been great men, and there have been great women. So why should you say that women aren't meant to do nothing else but cook and clean. That isn't right, and as far as I'm concerned, you need to take back that statement. If men can go out there and work, why cant women? Why shouldn't men cook and clean? Why......"

"Keep quiet and sit down my dear " Mr Aja said cutting her short. He said this while waving his hand and tightening his wrinkled face into a frown. Oroma didn't like the fact that she had been asked to shut up. She hated Mr Aja. Any further attempt to keep talking would look like disrespect, so she kept quiet till the class was over.

The incidence formed a good conversation for her and her gang. Esther had already heard the gist and was ready to shower him with insults in their discussion. She rushed to Art class with Onyi and Mimi, and sat beside Oroma. No one went closer when this four were together, and they never found the things they discussed normal or interesting. Oroma the fearless, Esther the sharp mouth, Onyi the fighter, and Mimi, the calmest but harshest. They talked about the issue all through their free period in class.

" Is that man mad?", Esther started. It was obvious that she took the slightest opportunities to raise an insult toward someone.

"Girl, calm down first. Let's hear the full gist na. Don't insult the man yet", Mimi said.

"Why shouldn't she...."Oroma began

"That man freaking said that women shouldn't do anything but cook and clean, so why are we in school then?"

"What else did he say?",Onyi asked.

"I can't remember" Oroma said waving her hand on the air.

"For me women aren't supposed to cook or clean sef. Its men that should do it.", Esther said.

"Correct", Oroma and Onyi said in agreement.

" No na. That's not right. Women can clean, but we shouldn't be limited to that alone.", Mimi said.

"See this stupid girl", Esther said

Oroma followed;

"Look, Mimi, women are better than men, so men should be the ones doing all the chores not us."

Mimi laughed shortly then said;

"No, You're getting this whole shit wrong. Feminism isn't about stating that women are better than men, but pushing for equality. I think you guys are crossing your bounds with your own statements oh. Men and women are human beings. Nobody is super, so we should all be given equal rights. Shikina."

Once Mimi finished talking, Oroma sighed, stood up from her chair and walked out of the class murmuring to herself. Onyi followed, and then Esther. But before Esther left, she said;

"You see you this girl, you dey talk nonsense too much."

    Although they quarreled openly like this, they still cared for each other. Once Onyi and Esther left, Oroma walked back in. Mimi was still sitting there.

She felt guilty because Mimi was making sense, but she wouldn't agree to be wrong after all. She'd add this to her diary once she got to the hostel. There was a lot more on her mind than she had said already. What she believed was that openly accepting wrongs was a total show of weakness.

CHAPTER TWO

Oroma sat alone in the reading hall solving her math assignment. Classes in school ran very fast this period. The math teacher, Mr john only gave many assignments without teaching since they had completed their scheme. Oroma ate lunch after school, slept for sometime, then came down stairs to finish the many math problems Mr John had given them. While she solved on and on, Mimi walked towards where she sat. She looked worried. On first thought, Oroma felt she was coming to solve the assignments with her as they usually did with the other girls, who were sleeping upstairs at the moment. But she looked too sad to be coming for such reason. She wasn't even with any notebook.

"Oroma can I talk to you about something?", Mimi asked looking downtrodden.

"Yes sure", she said returning her attention to her assignment.

"Oroma it's serious. Please stop solving for the meantime", Mimi said

"ok oh!!", Oroma exclaimed closing her math note.

"This is serious. What's the matter?"

"This thing I'm about to tell you eh, please don't tell anybody. I've been raped before. It was our houseboy, and I've been too ashamed to talk about this to anyone. It was painful. I was just 10 then. At least it'd have been better if it happened now that I'm 16. I didn't even know how to say it then.", Mimi started crying.

"I just felt like the whole world hated me cos even my mum didn't notice the way I became withdrawn. I've lived with this trauma up till this point, and that guy is somewhere enjoying life after causing me this emotional injury. You girls have been my pillars. Without you people in my life right now, maybe I'd have killed myself. But I've always been inspired by the three of you.", she said crying even more.

"Ah!! Is that why you're crying? You're a weakling. We've been talking about feminism in this school, and you're this weak. Abeg!!"

Oroma's statement made Mimi cry even more. The reading hall was empty since it was exclusively for the SS3 students, and many of them which included Oroma's friends were sleeping upstairs. This allowed Mimi to sob loudly. She had come to Oroma for advice and comfort, but she worsened her emotional condition instead. Mimi wasn't also one to keep quiet. She knew personally that Oroma just didn't get the point. She usually told herself that Oroma meant well, but just had the wrong perception about things.

"Look Oroma, I trusted that you were a friend. I came to you to seek comfort, but you've only made me feel worse. You are mean. I'm the only person who can tell you this cos everyone is scared of your arrogance. But not me. Asides this, please don't tell anybody what I've told you.", Mimi said and walked out very sad.

"See this idiot. You're weak. Keep deceiving yourself. Fool!!!!", Oroma let out. She believed she was right in this.

"A woman must be strong to face the barriers placed before her in life. A woman mustn't cry for the sake of a man. A woman must speak earlier when she's raped. What's even there sef. Every time people will be talking about stigma or trauma. Abeg free that talk. No matter what, me I'm strong oh!". she said this loudly as if talking to someone. She had memorized it, and said it usually to reaffirm her strength. This was her own way of waving off the painful words of Mimi.

Oroma went to meet her girls when she was done with her assignments. She was ready to bring up more and more funny jokes about their classmates that she had thought of, but she wouldn't mention Mimi's dilemma. That'd be wrong.

"Girls!!see eh!! Who has noticed the way Munachi walks?", Esther said chuckling.

" Omen!!!that guy walks like there's poo in his ass", Oroma said laughing hard.

Onyi and Mimi laughed along.

"No, no, the worst is Joseph", Mimi said standing up to demonstrate while laughing. They all laughed hard.

" And to think that he keeps gaping at nothing", Onyi added still laughing.

While they laughed on, one of their classmates, Cynthia, walked into the room with a plate in her hand.

"Mimi find me milk", she said with no politeness.

"I can't give you. It's remaining small, and can't you at least ask more politely?", Mimi said with the backing of the other girls who said in Unison;

"Don't mind her"

"See this stingy goat. Be claiming you don't have. Cow", Cynthia said looking up to the ceiling as if avoiding the faces of the other girls.

"Look at who's calling someone a Cow with your yam leg. ", Oroma said pointing at Cynthia's legs. They all laughed. Cynthia could only sigh, and walk out of the room. She was the one that made a mistake by attacking Mimi when she was with her gang.

Days in Crown International school ran as fast as usual. Oroma and her friends went about their normal dealings. They were happy kids. Mimi's secret was safe with Oroma. Although if Esther and Onyi knew about it, they'd also have told no one, but Mimi wouldn't be comfortable. So Oroma kept the secret. In fact, they never spoke about it again. But Oroma always wondered why Mimi should keep it a secret.

"What is she even scared of?", Oroma asked herself as she wrote on her diary almost everyday.

"Is it Stigma? What stigma? Is it Trauma? Which kind dirty trauma? I just wish she could be strong like me. If it's me, I'd have cut that boy's penis."

Her diary was her personal space. She could pour all her thoughts in here since no one came close to it. Who'd dare?

CHAPTER THREE

It was a Thursday evening, and everyone was out for sports already. Girls didn't stay together during sports. Oroma and her friends were given enough freedom to do things since they'd soon leave the school. This gave them the opportunity to talk with their boyfriends on the love benches around the field. Oroma had no boyfriend, but she'd usually sit with any guy that was with no girl, and talk about the weirdest things. Sometimes she spoke of her lovely grandmother, and other times about the way she feared her father. She just didn't have anything to talk about, and she was fondly called, Capless in Crown international school.

She wasn't in the mood to sit and talk on this day. A junior student had refused to fetch her water, and she was really vexed. She just walked to the school block, and rested her head on a desk in their empty class room. She wanted to stay away from others to enjoy the solitude of staying alone in school block during sports. She sat with inner satisfaction to have found a place as quiet as their class which was on the fourth floor with the principal's office. A class that could never be even half this quiet in the early time of the day when no teacher was around. She was happy that she had made a name up till this point of SS3. She was sure boys feared her, and none would have the gods to try her in anyway; especially sexually. There had been gists of boys coming to touch girls while they slept in school block, but she had never experienced it.

As she drowned in sleep while resting her head on the desk, she could feel a sweet sensation from hands of an obviously male figure. It seemed like a dream, and she'd wonderfully accept this advances in that dream if the figure was her spec. She looked up to grab the hand, and then realized she wasn't dreaming, but was rather wallowing in the fantasies of a real touch.

"Are you mad?", she said horrifically while throwing the hands of the Principal. She only realized it was him when she looked up to his face.

"Oh sorry sir", she said immediately believing that after all the man's touch wasn't for a reason of sex, and she had only thought too far. He was a man of pure dignity, a pastor, and too disciplined to think of such. Above all, he was the Principal. Why'd he think of doing such with her?

"No no. Calm down. You'll enjoy this", he said to her looking overly seductive for his person. Oroma wanted to shout. She didn't take rubbish from no man. But she never expected any advances from Principal. Maybe he wanted to teach her something like History, or just advice her on how to go about life. This man was just too much of a good man to do what she was thinking already. She really looked up to this man. He forcefully drew her out of the chair. He stared right into her eyes as if wanting to carelessly kiss her lips. She wanted to scream, but somehow her mouth couldn't open to it. What was about to go down scared her. The principal held her mouth, then took her to his office. He locked his door which stood directly opposite to her class. Now no one could come here. Even the teachers feared this office. He induced her to unconsciousness with his wide palm which fiercely pressed against her nostrils. He pulled his trouser and shirt, and threw them far with heavy thrust. He drew her sports short down. He was open to her inner self now. He did what he wanted to do. He got her bleeding within seconds of front and back movements. He wore his clothes back, and woke her up with aggressive kicks. She woke up to her pool of blood. It gushed out from in between her thighs. This was what confirmed her feminine dignity. This was what she reserved for her husband. She had imagined the lucky man unzipping her wedding gown from behind. She imagined him struggling with the high bump that stood on her back, perfectly completing her womanly curves. But now her imaginations had been shattered. She had been raped. She never knew this could happen to her, and now she had already proclaimed herself as a woman to stand for other women. How'd she be now? She didn't know.

"Take! Clean yourself up", the Principal said handing her a roll of tissue. She cried bitterly. Even her classmates hadn't seen her cry, but now she couldn't hold it. She cried for the sake of a man. This was what she said she would never do, but she couldn't hold these tears back. They were tears of real anguish and pain. How cruel of this man. She told herself she was strong everyday, but it was time to prove it. She couldn't believe she had been raped. She wanted to slap this man, but somehow she couldn't because of the respect she had for this man. No one would even believe principal raped her. He was a very good man, but in her eyes now, he was the devil himself.

She wiped the remaining blood on her legs. She could feel some kind of pain through her midsection. She walked slowly out of his office. She didn't look at his face at all. She didn't want any glimpse at the man who had defiled her. Oroma tried to ignore the pains she felt around her groins, and trekked the whole distance to her hostel without talking to anyone. She simply had her bath, got dressed up and laid on her bed. When Esther, Onyi and Mimi were back inside after sports, they expected Oroma to come join them in their latest mockery gist, but she didn't. They didn't bother disturbing her when they saw her lying down and looking sad on her bed. They just left her in her own space because they thought it was one of her usual mood swings.

Oroma also missed dinner that night. She kept sobbing quietly on her bed without letting anyone notice. All she kept imagining was how Principal had done it while she was unconscious. How mean of him. He could kill someone if given the chance. And later he'd preach in devotion ground about keeping God's word.

"What a two-faced man", she thought. She still didn't believe he had done this to her. "A pastor of a church. A man that wore baggy trousers that swept the floor. A man that doesn't permit examination malpractice. How possible?", she thought about these things and sobbed more.

Her thoughts then went to Mimi. How cruel of her to have told her that she was weak. Maybe Mimi was actually weak, and she was being equally weak. She wiped her tears immediately. She was the only person in the room at the time. She got up from her bed, and She spoke loudly;

"No! I can't be weak. Crying is for weaklings. At least I won't get into any trauma like that weak Mimi girl. Abeg let me allow this shit slide."

Oroma talked aloud like this when she was angry. She agreed to sleep this off, but before that, she wrote her feelings on her diary. It was her normal source of comfort, but this time she sobbed when she saw her write-up on her diary;

"A Woman Must Be Strong To Face The Barriers Placed Before Her In Life. A Woman Mustn't Cry For The Sake Of A Man. A Woman Must Speak Earlier When She's Raped. What's Even There Sef."

Her own words sounded absurd to her now, and it made her sob more. How'd she speak now that she was raped. It was all too shameful. She remembered how she had memorized this many times. How wrong had she been, and maybe she had been over doing this feminism stuff. It just dawned on her that after all maybe this wasn't her thing, and she had been forcing it with the wrong perceptions. Principal had opened her eyes.

When she was done, she laid back down on her bed, and closed her eyes to sleep. She still kept imagining that ugly man's body close to hers. It felt disgusting. This feeling kept hunting her through the night. She woke up at three different instances where she saw the Principal. It frightened her. Some how his imagery also scared her. She wished she could never see him again in her life. She just hated that evil man who had snatched the most precious part of her- HER VIRGINITY.

CHAPTER FOUR

Oroma was dressed very early for school the next day. She couldn't sleep in the night because of the strange nightmares she kept having. She decided to get up and bath with the time instead. This was unlike her who was known in the girls' hostel for her lateness in school preparations. The hostel mistress, Miss Aku usually had to chase her round the hostel with a cane because she was always late. But this day was different. Oroma was up and dressed by 6am. She didn't follow her girls to the toilet, or sit with them in the dinning. She instead sat alone by the right hand corner of the big dinning hall which contained over 100 female students. She kept staring at the table, and didn't stand on the queue for food. She had no appetite. Her girls became worried. They knew something was surely wrong with her. They walked together to where she sat in the dinning hall after they had finished their own meals.

"Come babe what happened na?", Onyi said in a worrisome tone. Oroma didn't reply. She just kept staring at the empty table in front of her.

"Wait oh, you've not eaten sef. What's happening na? You can tell us oh", Mimi added. Oroma only heaved a sigh. She didn't answer in words. She kept staring at the table like it was more important than their faces.

"I hear say she no chop yesterday. How possible? Oroma wey like food.", Esther said jokingly and laughed. Mimi and Onyi laughed as well. This was meant to trigger Oroma's mood, but it didn't. They continued trying.

"To think of it oh. She woke up before everybody", Mimi said and forced out a laughter to impress Oroma, but Oroma wasn't moved at all. The three girls went closer to her. Esther sat on the hard mahogany table while Onyi and Mimi remained standing. Esther reached for her chin in a girly manner, and said;

"Oromama talk to us na." They were really worried because Oroma could hardly remain sad unless something was really serious. Just like when she had been flogged in front of everyone in the school for what she didn't do. It saddened her, but she was sad for only one day. The girls were rest assured that whatever it was, it had to be serious.

Mimi and Onyi placed their hands on her back one after the other as if patting her. Mimi tried tickling her sides, but she wasn't responding.

"What's doing you sef? Nah you do pass?" Esther said annoyingly with her angry pidgin voice.

"You girls should just leave me alone abeg. Did I call you here?" Oroma spoke out fiercely. Immediately, she stood up and went to another chair. The girls new best not to disturb her. At least they had done their bests as friends.

"Oroma it's devotion time oh! Won't you come?", Mimi asked. Oroma still didn't reply. The three girls walked to school leaving Oroma alone in the dinning hall.

Oroma began to sob again. She didn't attend devotion because she didn't want to see the face of the Principal. She didn't know why. Was it fear? Was it hatred for his deceit? She knew he'd be preaching about avoiding immorality now. How ironic? The same man that defiled her preaching about Immorality and self control. She despised him.

Oroma rested her head on her desk while in class. She didn't go round interloping in people's discussions like always. She didn't answer whoever talked to her. Her girls had come again, they kept annoyingly knocking on her desk, but she acted like nothing was happening. She acted as if she was numb to what was happening around her. It vexed all of them, and they returned to their class. Oroma didn't take part in any argument that came up that day. A mischievous boy, Ayo had said;

"Girls shouldn't be in school." Everyone was aware of what this could propel in Oroma, but Ayo tried testing her. To everyone's uttermost surprise, she didn't respond. She just kept mute and acted like no one had said anything. In fact, It all seemed like she didn't hear it, and that was what everyone chose to believe. All she did was switch positions from resting her head to sitting upright and crossing her arms.

As teachers came in and out, she didn't participate in their classes. All she did was stare at their faces. Even when the CRS teacher, Mr. Ugo said that women are meant to be like domestic slaves in the home, Oroma didn't raise her hand up. She didn't stir up an argument as usual. Everyone was surprised, but somehow they were happy that they could enjoy peace and be free from Oroma's unending arguments in art class and beyond. Her other girls formed feminist as well, but they didn't argue with teachers like her, and didn't talk a lot about it like her. She was just far much of a committed feminist than them.

Oroma slowly started to drown in personal sorrow. Days passed, and weeks came by without her mentioning this to anyone. Only her diary knew about this. She cried every night in the absence of people's eyes. She hardly read these days. She wondered why she couldn't tell anyone. Even her mum didn't know, and this prompted her choice of telling no one at all. To her, if mummy couldn't know, not even her girls should. Not even Mimi that told her about her own rape incidence. It all dawned on her that she was a rape victim. It was hard to accept the fact, but she still kept wallowing in the misery of thinking about it. She was sinking. For the passed weeks, she had stopped talking to people. She didn't come out for sports. She only walked from her room in her hostel to her class in school block or to the dinning for food. She only read sometimes in the midnight after much crying. She ate only the foods she loved too well. The incidence had made her selective as well. She didn't attend devotion. She didn't attend Sunday church services. She avoided every place that Principal could be in preaching a gospel that he secretly didn't practice. She was scared of him. She had stopped calling herself strong on her diary notes. She started accepting that she was weak. After all, she cried everyday. After all, she hadn't spoken of her own rape case. This was her own depiction of weakness, and she had been portraying it. But another thing that bothered her was if she was facing trauma. Was this how trauma felt? So she was actually weak. She just didn't know what to think about, and when to think about it. Her diary became a soil for planting words that never bore fruits in her. They only worsened her situation. Her own words annoyed her when she went through the damned book. She cried every single day. Her eyes were tired of producing tears. She needed to talk to someone, but she didn't know who'd be the best. She needed help, and she knew it.

Oroma was having a lonely period in her life. She had fallen sick twice, and at first had thought she was pregnant with Principal's child. But her monthly flow didn't stop. So, she knew it was sickness from too much brain stress. Her mental health was suffering. Her girls had done their bests, and no longer tried. They continued their friendship, but without Oroma. Only Mimi seemed more concerned, and suspicious, but her primal knowledge of Oroma's person made her think otherwise. Oroma was alone in this fight.

CHAPTER FIVE

Six months passed, and Oroma had told no one about what happened. They had gone home on holiday and returned, yet her mood was still the same. While at home her parents didn't think anything was wrong. Her mum had asked;

"Is everything ok?", But this was her mum's normal question. Of course she replied;

"Yes!"

"What else would mummy want to hear after all?", she asked herself in her diary. Oroma blamed her parents more, for not noticing something very serious was wrong with her. They just believed she was acting withdrawn in order to concentrate and read for her upcoming exams.

Oroma had started watching Comedic films. She thought they'd help her situation, but they didn't. She laughed for jokes that weren't meant to be funny. She looked pale. Her parents, Mr and Mrs Uzo had called her pale-look a good thing. They had said proudly that she was really putting in the work to make them proud by reading. They didn't know there was more to it. They hadn't noticed that she wasn't her usual warring self. With time Oroma began to feel like everyone had let her down. She felt the world hated her. Her parents didn't understand her as she thought they did. They commended something like looking pale which made her more angry. But even with this anger, she didn't speak up. Her closest friends no longer rolled with her. Although she hadn't given them the chance, but they should have continued trying. As far as she was concerned, only Mimi was worthy of being called a friend because she kept checking on her every single day although without talking to her. She usually came, and looked at her for short minutes then walked away. They should have stood by her anyway. She blamed people for virtually everything that went wrong in her life. She had stopped talking to everyone. She didn't even greet teachers or hostel mistresses. Teachers and students noticed the way she became withdrawn. She had been a thorn on their flesh, and so they appreciated the way she was now. They believed it was best for everyone. They were oblivious to the fact that it was about to kill her.

On this very Saturday, Oroma didn't go out at all. Saturday was usually a day when girls stayed out, played, talked with boys, danced in the hall, and so on. She was the only girl in the hostel. She was having the worst thoughts. She wanted to end it all. She wanted to free herself from all the hate in the world. She wanted to escape the pressure of thinking too much. She was tired of sharing the same earth with the man that took her best possession. It was either to die or to kill him, but the latter seemed more impossible. She resolved to die.

Oroma walked to the hostel mistress's house door. She peeped through the window close to it to see if anyone was in front of the hostel downstairs. No one was there. It was a good time. She pushed the door to check if it was open. She had watched when Mrs Aku walked out of the hostel for evening church service. Her main aim was to get a knife, and stab herself, but she was scared of the pain. She'd take the pain anyway. As far as she'd be free forever. The pain was too much. She searched the flat which contained a bedroom and a kitchen, but she didn't see any knife in the kitchen. She kept searching. She moved fast. As she searched, she prayed in her heart for God to forgive her sins. She prayed that He'd have mercy over her for what she was about to do. She checked the drawers in the kitchen. She opened every bucket, but didn't see it. While she was checking the top of the refrigerator, she saw a sniper bottle on the floor. It was boldly written;

"DON'T DRINK. FOR HOUSE RODENTS ONLY. " She didn't care. All that rang in her head was;

"What an easier way!"

She took the bottle of insecticide, and ran out of Miss Aku's flat.

She stood with the sniper in her room for minutes. She was still scared of what she was about to do. She was in tears. She believed it'd be her last tears, so she cried more and more. She held the bottle while her hand shook from fear. She went on her kneels. She wished Mummy could run in here now, and save her. She wished her and her mum had that much bond. She wished her girls could come to her rescue. That's if they still cared about her. Why did everyone hate her? Why was she so uncared for?

She took a dangerous sip.

While she was still on her kneels waiting for the sniper to do it's work on her, Mimi walked in. As soon as she entered, Oroma fell with a force that seemed like she was tipsy. But she wasn't. The effect of the sniper was coming through. Mimi's eyes got opened in shock when she saw what Oroma was holding. She was even more shocked when she saw Oroma was crying. No one had ever seen her like this. But that wasn't the main problem. Oroma was about to die.

"Mimi! Mimi!", Oroma exclaimed. Her voice was shrill. She sounded much calmer than when she sleep talked. It was serious. Mimi had never seen her like this before.

"He raped me. He raped me".

Mimi heard what she said. Many things ran through her mind, but the best thing was to save her life first. Everything could come next. Mimi ran out of the room. She returned with some boys to carry Oroma. She was crying now too. She pitied her friend. And she had been raped? The warrior had been raped? The one she looked up to had been raped? Oroma would definitely explain if she survived this. But would she survive?

The school bus was ready. They moved Oroma to a hospital close to the school. She was still breathing. The doctors took charge. They put her in an emergency room. Mimi was the only student in the hospital. While Oroma was being treated upon, Mimi prayed. She prayed for God to save the life of her friend. Her and other girls had been bad friends. How didn't they notice she had been raped? Who could have raped Oroma?

"Where's my daughter?", Oroma's mum asked in a loud voice. She was already in tears. She had no make up on. She was wearing a blue jean and a big white shirt. She didn't even wear a wig. She came with her unbraided natural hair which wasn't combed. She was in shatters because of fear for the life of her daughter.

"She's being attended to inside there ma", Mimi answered pointing to the emergency ward room. She said nothing else. Even though Oroma's mum kept asking;

"What happened to her na?"

Mimi didn't know how to tell a mother that her loving daughter had been raped. Yes! she had only that information from the last words of Oroma, but how'd it sound to the ears of Oroma's mum. Even when she had been raped, she didn't speak up. In fact, Oroma was the only person that knew till date. Mimi remembered Oroma's reply that day. She remembered her words against tears of a raped woman. But she had seen Oroma in that state some minutes ago. She needed to know who had broken the unbreakable woman, Oroma.

CHAPTER SIX

Mimi slept in the hospital with Mrs. Uzo. She didn't know how she had dosed off on the hospital's uncomfortable waiting room chair. It was really hard, but anything for her friend. She was very worried about her. Oroma's dad came very early the next morning. That was when the doctor came out of the ward. It had taken so long. All they wanted to hear was good news that she was alive and well. The doctor wasn't smiling. He came out, and asked;,

"Where are Oroma Uzo's parents?"

Oroma's parents got up immediately. The doctor motioned for them to follow him into his office which had a white door, and stood adjacent to the exit door. They all sat. The doctor began;

"She made it", with a slight grin on his face. Her mum shouted;

"Praise God!" While her dad just smiled, and shook hands with the doctor.

The doctor continued;

"It was hard. There were complications, but we're grateful to God that she came out victorious. Your daughter had a poisonous substance in her system, and from the explanation that was given to us by the girl out there on the hazard emergency form she filled yesterday, she had drank an insecticide intentionally. It seems like she wanted to take her life. Please in whatever you do after now, just ensure you watch your daughter."

Oroma's parents were quiet in shock. Their only child had tried to commit suicide. It sounded absurd. What must have gone wrong that they didn't know. They'd ask her.

After the doctor permitted all of them to go in, they all rushed in. Oroma was lying down on the hospital bed. A drip was connected to her wrist. She was awake, but obviously weak.

"My baby…", Mrs Uzo started.

"Don't worry. I'll tell you everything", Oroma said cutting her short.

"Ok. Oya you go outside first." Miss Uzo said dismissing Mimi.

"No mummy. Let her stay." Oroma said.

"OK na. If you please", her mum said finally. Mr Uzo just leaned on the wall. He wasn't much of a talker.

"About six months ago, I went to the school block to rest my angry head in the evening. While I was sleeping, Principal came, and started touching me." Everyone's mouth was wide open in shock.

"Your principal?", Mr. Uzo asked.

"Yes daddy. He pressed my nostrils till I fell unconscious. When I woke up, I was bleeding. I had been raped." Her mum was crying already. Mimi just looked at her like she was an unsolvable puzzle. She was definitely sad for her friend, but this wasn't the strong person she knew. Her dad was walking back and forth now. He was rubbing his hands, and was furiously thinking of how to deal with the Principal.

"Mimi please don't tell anybody about this. At least not yet. ", Oroma said finally.

"You have my word.", Mimi said. Although she said this, her mind wasn't at peace. This was the same Oroma that called trauma a weak person's thing. But she was strong na. This was the same person that said whoever was raped should speak earlier, but she had kept this for six months. It was comparably short sha, but only before her suicide attempt. She had been more affected because she tried suicide. The strong Oroma wasn't strong after all.

Mr. Uzo filed a case against the Principal. The cunning man hired a lawyer for himself. Oroma told her dad's lawyer everything that had happened. She was pampered, and given excessive attention. It started to disgust her, but it was better than being left out anyway. Oroma wasn't sure that all she had told the lawyer was enough to put the Principal in jail, but she hoped he'd pay for his crime.

On the day of his trial, Oroma sat in the front sit with her mum. Her secret was open now, and she felt so ashamed about it. She was still melancholic. She hadn't regained herself. Everyone was talking about it. She was sure that even if Mimi didn't talk about it in school, people would have heard the gist. She'd become a laughing stock. That's if she'll return to the school anyway. WAEC was two months away. She wanted to get this over with, write the exams, and Japa, as the Yoruba cleaners would say. It meant run/escape.

Oroma's lawyer won the case, but he had won it at the expense of Oroma's already weakened emotions. She was made even sadder by it.

First, the fact that she was raped was known by everybody. The court proceedings were even covered by AIT. She had become known for this. People started using it to get likes on their useless posts through hashtags. She had seen one of them on Instagram. A girl posted a picture of herself with her mouth covered by the hands of a man from behind. The girl wrote beneath;

"#justice for Oroma."

It vexed Oroma that she had to be the Oroma that they were referring to on a popular rape incidence. She had posted many activist pictures of other girls who had been raped and needed justice in the past, but she didn't know they felt like she did now. She wouldn't do it ever again.

Second, she had felt like a weakling when she surprisingly saw Esther and Onyi stand to testify against the Principal. They had been raped by him too. But they didn't try to kill themselves. They never got withdrawn from their usual selves. Oroma began to see herself as the actually weak one. She started to write on her diary from that day that she was the weakest person on earth and no one else. She started telling her diary that she should have died instead of seeing the level of weakness she possessed. But the girls hadn't spoken up since until that day. They hadn't told her. They were ashamed too. Probably, she wasn't the only weak one, but she believed her weakness was greater than theirs. She believed it was greater than anybody's.

She just kept writing on her diary;

"Why me? Why me?"

CHAPTER SEVEN

Oroma became the talk of the whole school. It made her feel very ashamed. Her school had been so dumb to openly announce the offence of the already convicted principal. They didn't care about the emotional and psychological effects it could have on the victim. This pushed Oroma more downwards. She was sadder than before. She believed that even her school didn't care about her emotions. She believed no one did. She was still in a world of her own with her diary. She was going to school from home now. This was because the doctor had asked her parents to watch her in order to avoid further attempts to take her life. Oroma hadn't regained her warring self back. She missed herself.

Mrs. Uzo had been thoughtful to place Oroma for therapy. She gave her only child all the attention she needed in the world and even more. She stopped going to work just so that she could place an eye on Oroma. While she did all these, she noticed her daughter wasn't still out of her melancholy. She waited till it was holiday time, and enrolled Oroma for therapy. It was a good idea. She took Oroma to the place after many days of "you must go! I won't go" quarreling.

Oroma was left alone with the woman who seemed like someone that observed everything on her body. Had she heard about what happened? Why'd her parents be going around telling people about such thing?

"Good afternoon.", Oroma said not forgetting her manners.

"Afternoon darling", the obviously nice woman said. She had a glowing lip gloss on. Oroma loved to see women with lip gloss. She believed it gave them confidence, and now she wanted it.

"Wow! I love your lip gloss's shine. What's the name. I'd love to have it."
Once she said this, the woman who wore a corporate white shirt, opened a
drawer and handed her the lip gloss. Oroma was more than thankful.

"Oh my God! Thank you so much." They hadn't started a conversation on
the main reason she was here, but she already liked her. While at home
when her mum told her she was enrolled for therapy, she had imagined a
grumpy old man as the therapist. But here she was thanking a young and
beautiful lady for giving her a lip gloss she admired. It had a spare stick in
it, so she didn't bother thinking about using the same stick with her new
friend.

"So let's get down to business Darling. Do you mind?", the woman asked
so nicely. She spoke in a tone that already softened the heart of Oroma.
She'd tell her everything. She'd tell her about the rape incidence and
about her personal problems. She'd tell her that she called her self strong
everyday, but had proven to be weak. She'd tell her about Mimi, and what
she said to her that still haunted her now. She'd tell her about her feminist
principles. She'd show her her diary. She'd let her in to her real self that
even her parents hadn't been let into. She'd really tell her everything. It
was time to make a new friend, and yes! Return to the original Oroma.
Nothing would stop her. No more shame. No more crying. No more
weakness.

"Let's get to it ma", Oroma said smiling so widely.

"OK, I love your smile.", The woman said. Oroma felt more delighted

"And by the way, don't call me ma. That's old baby. Call me something
sweet that you can chose by yourself, but my name is Nancy." Oroma was
more impressed by her show of youthfulness.

"Ok. I'll call you Nany hun. If that soothes you" Oroma said still smiling widely. She felt like she was talking with her real girlfriends in school. She still hadn't reunited with them. After these sessions, she would.

"Yeah. That's pretty girl, and I'll just call you caramel cos your complexion is just as dark and shiny." Nancy said finally. Oroma was ready to stay with her forever. She was just too nice.

"Alright. So I was raped by my Principal in school about 7months ago." Oroma started. She talked about this with so much ease as if she had been touched by God. She usually said this, and broke into tears in the process, but Nancy had changed it within seconds. This meant that she could help her regain herself faster. She'd stick with Nancy.

"After I tried committing suicide, the secret leaked, and he was convicted for his crime. I'm still a very sad person don't mind that I'm happy today."

"Is that all you'll like to tell Nany hun?", Nancy asked with a childish stare.

"No there's more."Oroma said looking sad this time. She was no longer looking at Nancy's face. It was time to say things she had never said before. Nancy was quick to jack a pen and a jotter. She knew it was time for the real deal.

"I always told myself that I was strong everyday. I've stood as a feminist in school, and I believe that that needs so much strength and strong will. Before this incidence, I never cried for a man. I saw that as weakness. I mean, why should I cry for a man? Those tears disgusted me. But since that incidence, I've cried virtually everyday. I feel like a weakling, and its making me sadder. I also saw my friends in court during the trial of My Principal. They had been raped too. I felt like they were far stronger than me that keeps claiming to be strong. They had been raped, but they didn't face trauma like me. Yes! Trauma is for the weak, and I'm weak. Apart from that, I think women are better than men, and I just want a society where men should do all that they want women to do. It bothers me everyday that people call this my thought absurd. They don't even want to know my line of direction. All they want is to support those demons who perpetuate so much evil with what stands in between their legs. That isn't all aunty Nancy." Oroma broke into tears.

"This is the worst. I've felt guilty about this for a longtime now. There's a girl. We were very close. Her name is Mimi. We even had a gang which involved Esther and Onyi that I saw in court. She told me she had been raped. She told me this about a month before I was raped. But I didn't talk to her calmly. I called her a weakling. I insulted her, and now see me. Who's the weak one? I even feel more guilty because she's the one that saved my life when I was trying to commit suicide. I can't apologize to her. Accepting wrongs is for weak people. Everything is just on my head. " She said finally scratching her head as if something was itching her badly while she cried more.

"Caramel, you are strong and beautiful. Stop crying baby. Well, personally, I feel you want to let me know more", Nancy said

"Truth be told, I do. But I can't remember everything now. The best thing would be to give you my diary. I write there everyday. Its updated, and it contains everything that has happened to me this year." Oroma said finally wiping her tears with her handkerchief.

"Wow! You have a diary? That's hot babe. Please bring it tomorrow if you don't mind." Nancy said.

"Sure, I will". Oroma said.

"I guess we should take a break now baby. We'll continue tomorrow, and trust me, you're getting there. Aren't you hungry?" Nancy asked.

"Oh yes, I am. I'll get something once you dismiss me".

"No you don't have to", Nancy said opening the same drawer the lip gloss came out from. She brought out 5 snickers chocolate packs, and handed them to Oroma, then she took one for herself from inside the drawer. Did she plan this all out? How did she know Oroma loved snickers? How did she know she loved glowing lip gloss? She was an angel.

Oroma totally enjoyed the session with Nancy. In fact, on the second day, she was ready to go again before her mum had dressed up. It was surprising to Mrs. Uzo, but she was happy to have seen Oroma smile today. Oroma got the diary, and gave it to Nancy once they got there. She was disappointed when Nancy told her they wouldn't talk, and that she had to give her one day to go through everything and give her feed back. But Oroma looked up to that day. She missed Nancy.

On the day of the scheduled session with Nancy, Oroma wore the shiny lip gloss on her lips. She wanted to impress Nancy with it. During the session, Nancy spoke nicely as usual, and Oroma admired her. Above all, Nancy had the key to Oroma's real person. She was ready to unlock it.

"Baby, I'll say things rapidly like you the other day oh. You know you didn't even pause that day. You were just talking fast". Nancy said laughing. Oroma laughed too.

"Be as fast as you can. I'm a good listener".

"Alright. First of all, your Principal is a very bad man, but don't judge all men by the singular act of a wicked man. There are many sweet men out there Darling, and trust me you'd love to meet my husband". Nancy said this and paused intentionally.

"You have a husband? Wow! That's nice". Oroma said quickly. She was shocked that Nancy was married, and was still so youthful.

"Yes baby. Let me continue. I want to get something clear to you. Being strong doesn't mean you can't cry. Crying is normal. Being strong doesn't mean you can't face trauma. Of course rape is bad, but trauma could come since the victims keep thinking about it. Even the strongest person in the world can face trauma. It isn't a criteria for judging strength, and trust me baby, from all I've seen in you, You're a very strong girl. As for your friends, they may be facing trauma, but act as if they aren't sad on the outside. Remember don't judge a book by its cover. They may be going through the worst emotional situation, but you just can't see it, so don't think you're weak cos of that. Like I said, you're very strong. Should I pause or should I continue?" Nancy asked.

"No continue. I grab everything you're saying, and I'm enjoying it." Oroma was really enjoying it. Nancy wasn't reading from any paper, and she had all these coming from herself. Oroma found this amazing, and would harken to her every word.

"Darling, men aren't better than women, and women aren't better than men. This is exactly what true feminists try to let people understand. I'm not saying you're a bad feminist. In fact, I'm happy you're strong willed and ready to take on the world, but you should stop seeing women as better than men. Just see it like this. Men and women are human beings. That is why women shouldn't be limited to kitchen or their households. That is why women shouldn't be made to pass through circumcision. That's why women should be allowed to go to school. Feminists want equity. They don't want superiority. Instead, they ask for men to reduce their level of superiority and embrace equity as well as change their perception of masculinity. I hope you get me". Nancy said.

"Yes I do. Go on." Oroma said. She was really enjoying this. And she was picking up many things.

"Finally, about your friend Mimi, just apologize to her. Accepting wrongs isn't weakness. In fact it's a show of courage to accept mistakes. Many big people in the world can't do this, and it shows that they're weak and cowardly. I know you're none of those, so from now on, in whatever you do, remember to accept when you're wrong, and take correction. It'll build you. That'd be all". Nancy said, and heaved a loud sigh of relief. She had talked for so long.

"Thankyou", Oroma said shortly.

"Do you care for some almond nuts?", Nancy asked.

"Yes please", Oroma said happily. She was really pondering on all Nancy had said. It really was time. It was time for her to return to herself. And not just herself, but her refined self.

CHAPTER EIGHT

After the session with Nancy, Oroma began to see life from a whole different angle. She had grabbed everything sweet Nancy told her, and was ready to make a change. Yes! she had been wrong about many things, but any human being could be wrong. We just have to accept our mistakes. Oroma was thinking about her life. She decided to write everything in her diary. At least to correct the old things she had written. She started;

"I've been wrong all along. I've believed and lived by many wrong principles and perceptions. It's time to change. It's time to be a better me. First, it isn't weakness to accept when you're wrong. In fact, it's a show of courage and bravery. It's a show of humility also. Men aren't super, and women aren't super. We're all human beings, and we're supposed to speak for each other when need be. Women aren't supposed to be limited to the kitchen, and men too. We're all meant to be given equal opportunities to achieve whatever we want in life. Facing trauma after rape or bullying isn't weakness. It's purely human. But this doesn't go to say that rape is good, or bullying should be accepted. Speaking about rape, men shouldn't be justified to have raped because a girl wears something short. After all girls that cover their whole bodies also get raped. I must fight this. We're all meant to treat each other nicely, advice each other properly, and be good to one another. Discrimination against anyone shouldn't be permitted. It could damage the social and emotional condition of people, and so should be grossly avoided. We also shouldn't allow the words of people to define us. In fact, that is the true weakness. So I will be strong. No! I am strong. This time my strength doesn't mean that I can't cry or face trauma. It means I can cry, but have a reason for crying. It means I can face trauma, but fight it hard and come out of it. It means I'm to speak truth to power, and speak of the injustices in my immediate society. It means I must say the truth even if I stand alone."

Oroma paused from writing to go get a chocolate pack from the fridge in her room. Her room was girly, but tough girly. Instead of having pictures and paintings of the red and blue powerpuff girls, she had that of the green. She was the toughest. Instead of having pink colored paint in her room, she had purple. Everything mattered to her now. Even the look of her room. The way it was now gave her a deep sense of strength and power. She had asked for a refurbishing of her room only days ago. She needed it for confidence.

Oroma finished the chocolate in no time, and she got back to write..

"The world isn't mean or wicked, but many people in it are. Some people are still good. We must sort for this some, and surround ourselves with them. It'll build us better. There are many people with wrong perceptions and ideologies in the world. Our immediate society needs help from dangers of stereotypes, wrong cultural beliefs, and so on. I must change them. I must try my best to help people have better ideologies concerning themselves and others. Many women of our time are brought up with the perception that they're to grow and depend on a husband for everything. They grow with the notion that they can't be complete without men, and so must learn to cook and clean to please a man. They're told to limit their achievements to avoid intimidating a man. These must be changed. Women can achieve like men. Why not? As for Mimi, I'll apologize to her once we resume school. She's a nice person. I had said mean things to her, but I'll apologize. Apologizing is a form of acknowledging mistakes, and that's one of the things I want to achieve. I also want to reunite with my girls, and hear their stories properly. I'm now in a better place to advice them. We'll be the best feminists together. Finally diary, I want to be a Lawyer to shaken my world better. I hope it comes through well."

Oroma felt satisfied to have corrected all the wrongs that had entered that book. She believed that if the diary was corrected, she was corrected. She felt very fulfilled and happy. She stayed for some time staring at the ceiling, and then she slept off. It was a sleep to the end of her old self.

CHAPTER NINE

Mr. and Mrs. Uzo were shocked at how quickly Oroma regained herself. They were more shocked at how often she smiled now. It all seemed like a miracle. Mrs. Uzo wanted to host a Thanksgiving in their church, but she was stopped by Mr. Uzo. He didn't want any publicity that could take Oroma back to her downtrodden self.

Once the holiday was over, Oroma returned to school. She no longer came from home. She was happy to be back here where it all started, but even happier to be back here as a new person- not the Oroma they knew. She loved looking around, but she was disgusted by the way everyone kept staring at are. Definitely they looked at her like that because they all knew she had been raped. But this didn't bother her much. She always said to herself;

"What's the most they can do? Mock me? That won't change anything."

When she got to the girls' hostel, she rushed to the room where her and her girls usually stayed. She didn't bother arranging her things into her locker yet. She just wanted to start talking with them, so that they could see she had changed.

"Babes how far", she said as she entered the room.

"Yayyyyyyyyyyy!", the other three girls echoed in unison. This was how they welcomed people in their hostel.

"How's it been with all of you na"

"Fine oh", "Ok", "just there", the three girls replied differently.

"Omo make ona arrange fast. Plenty gist dey", Oroma said walking out of the room and laughing. They all laughed along and rushed to finish arranging things so that they could gist. They knew whenever there was plenty gist coming, there was plenty laughter too.

When they had all finished packing, they gathered together, and started talking. They enjoyed each other's company again. Oroma apologized to Mimi openly while they discussed. They also talked about all their rape incidences, and Oroma gave them the advice she had planned. They were more than happy. Their relationship became realer because they now knew the deepest secrets that they had hidden from each other all along. The girls talked till about 10pm, and they agreed to go and make cereal, and also eat together. They contributed the needed materials.

"I'll bring milk", one said

"I'll bring Milo"

"I'll bring corn flakes. The soaks must be large oh", Oroma said. They referred to made cereal as soaks.

While they poured things into the bowl plate, Ella walked into the room with another plate. She was known in the whole hostel for begging too much. Once they saw her with a bowl plate, they knew what she was coming for. But they were shocked. They were shocked because it was the first day. She swung her long hair from right to left as she walked. She was very popular in the school, but hated in the hostel because of her begging.

"You guys oh. Please give me milk". Ella said.

"Ah! Ah! Even on first day?", Esther asked rhetorically.

"Me sef no know oh", Oroma said.

"Ah!", Mimi let out.

"mhmmm."Onyi made this sound with a shrug.

"If you don't want to give me, just say so". Ella said

"We don't want to na". Oroma said laughing. Her girls laughed as well. They all knew that Ella had her own provisions, but wouldn't open it till that of everyone else was finished.

"See these useless girls. And you this Oroma with your sharp mouth. Abi it has been cut now. Rape gang". Ella said, and sighed. She had called them a rape gang because they had all been raped. The gist had gone far. Oroma got up. Mimi, Esther and Onyi thought she'd start a fight like the normal Oroma would, but she didn't.

"Look Ella or whatever they call you. It's sad that you keep wallowing in poverty, and managing the little provision that you have. We that have, we're eating well. Go and beg the whole hostel. Witch. You're calling us rape gang because we've all been raped. But you're the same girl that goes about giving yourself to boys like a prostitute. Whore." Oroma said all these to Ella. Her words came out swiftly, and the way her girls laughed afterwards made Ella start to cry. She had brought this upon herself. She was known in the whole school for how she did immoral things, and now it had been used against her. She felt bad, but she had caused this. She was trying to weaken them with their unfortunate rape, but it backfired.

She walked out of the room in tears. The girls laughed more and more.

"This one na correct gist for another day', Esther said laughing harder.

"I swear ", Mimi said

"No oh! She for come back. See her mouth like rape gang. But that name sweet oh! We could call ourselves rape gang since we're against rape." Onyi said and continued laughing.

"Na only you ya. How'd we answer rape gang?" Oroma said laughing, and pushing Onyi's head.

"What about sisters?". Mimi asked with her normal low tone.

"That's way better", Oroma said.

"I agree." Onyi said

"Me too". Esther said finally.

They agreed to call their group, sisters, and by so doing, they agreed to stand by each other forever like real sisters.

CHAPTER TEN

It was overly noticeable now that Oroma had changed. Her wrong principles had been corrected, and her personality was improved. Her and her gang members could walk more confidently now with a #feminist high shoulder in their school. They could discuss matters more openly and more wisely. They had all experienced the same thing although at different times. Onyi and Esther had been raped in JSS3 by the same Principal and at the same time. They narrated to Oroma how he had given them poisoned pies, and they dosed off after eating it. They woke up after sometime, and saw themselves bleeding. They agreed to tell no one about it, but after they saw that they could help in putting the Principal behind bars, they spoke up! They were originally ashamed of saying it, but now felt very free after speaking up.

"Thank God we've spoken up oh. Now my heart can be free." Esther had said while they talked in the room.

The girls had more unity. They gained more power. They understood the menace of rape better now, and believed that all that had happened, happened to give them a wider knowledge on how to tackle it. As always, they were called the weirdest girls in school. This was because they kept seriously discussing issues concerning the society instead of the usual teenage talks of music stars and actors. They loved themselves nevertheless.

Oroma woke up early these days. It wasn't a bad thing. She attended social gatherings like before, and engaged in petty arguments about social life of women. She resumed what she was known for, which was arguing with teachers while lessons went on. But something was different. The thing was that the teachers, themselves, began to share in her views, and understand what she was saying. They began to agree with her unlike before when they never agreed with any point she made. Even Mr Aja who she hated dearly had listened to her on their latest argument. He had said;

"Yes! That's a sensible point. You're correct. We're all human my dear."

She was delighted when he said this. At least she had won the most difficult heart she knew.

She was more dogged about her principles now. She was more than ready to speak for women, and so were her girls. She believed that the breeding ground for fighting this issue was in her close environment. She didn't have to wait till she was all grown to make a change. She just told herself always that change begins with her, and there's no time to waste.

Oroma accepted her wrongs easily now. She said sorry even when it wasn't warranted. Everyone became more comfortable around her, but they always knew to watch their statements, or face the rot of the warring Oroma. She cried when she was pained, and laughed when she was meant to. She played much, but was still a feminist.

Oroma became more accepted. She was given a listening ear. She was happy every day. She smiled more commonly. She talked with boys more often. This was all she wanted, but didn't know how to get. All thanks to sweet Nancy, Oroma started calling herself strong again, and this time, it was a real strength.

Printed by Books on Demand GmbH, Norderstedt / Germany